ACCOUNTABILITY AMONG MEN

ACCOUNTABILITY AMONG MEN

BOB BELTZ

Gary J. Oliver, Ph.D., General Editor

MOODY PRESS
CHICAGO

ISBN: 0-8024-3716-8

1 3 5 7 9 10 8 6 4 2

Printed in the United States of America

On a crisp Saturday night in Denver, Don maneuvered his dark blue Buick slowly down a seamy stretch of East Colfax Avenue. Don's eyes scanned up and down the street like those of a predator seeking its prey, as he sought a lady of the night to satisfy his uncontrollable lust.

In truth, Don loathed his habit, and self-condemnation accompanied these late-night journeys into the city; but usually he could block such feelings from his consciousness with these strong desires of the flesh. After all, no one would know and no one would ask this independent man.

Don's routine was always the same: Find a teenage prostitute and head for one of the cheap motels further out on Colfax where other "respectable" men from the suburbs would also be living out their secret lives. The prostitute would be no older than his own daughter, and the great fear of his life was that some day one of these young girls would recognize him in public and reveal his hypocrisy and duplicity.

But Don's sense of wrong was greater tonight, for tomorrow would be Sunday, and he would be serving communion at church with the rest of the deacons. Somewhere deep inside he longed for deliverance from this life of shame. But tonight the desire drove him on. A voice in his head kept reassuring, "No one will know, no one will know!" But another voice, at a level much deeper, reminded him that there was always One who knew.

How can some men live with such inconsistencies? All too frequently, Christian men find spiritual, moral, and ethical defeat in their lives and don't know how to change. In the 1990s, we are hearing of more government, business, and, yes, even Christian leaders who have been living double lives. For that matter, many Christian men struggle to maintain integrity at work, at home, and at play.

Most want to change their patterns but don't know how. If we try to spot the causes of their inconsistencies, we'd find that men fail for many reasons. The reasons range from indifference to God and inconsistent or nonexistent prayer and devotional times to anger, illness, and even fatigue. Though a better prayer and devotional life will help, resolving a basically spiritual problem often requires more for men who, because of fear, egoism, or cultural expectations, try to move through life alone. Men need to be accountable to other men.

My hunch is that if we could unravel all the strands of human experience leading to such incredible contradiction we might find one common thread: a lack of accountability. Being accountable helps men to recognize that their actions have consequences and to have both the courage and assistance to find lives of consistency.

My Brother's Keeper

Rugged individualism. We are told that it made America great. That is a culturally created fiction, yet it is an image that most men in our culture emulated while growing up. I remember Saturday mornings, sitting in front of my grandma's TV, watching the Lone Ranger and wishing I could be like him. It never dawned on me that without Tonto, his faithful Indian companion, he would usually have been in deep trouble. Even the Lone Ranger needed a friend to help fight those cattle rustlers and the other outlaws he would face. "*Kimosabe,* look out!"

One of the earliest men to walk our planet, Cain also was a rugged individualist. His brother Abel was a man of faith (Hebrew 11:4). Though many believe Cain become enraged with Abel because of simple jealousy, I believe that Abel tried to hold Cain accountable and that Cain rebelled against duty and being held accountable for his actions. Jesus declared that Abel was a prophet. (Luke 11:50–51).

Cain's words to God, "Am I my brother's keeper?" (Genesis 4:9) suggest Cain wasn't "into" accountability. The result? He murdered his brother and spent the rest of his days living in the Tombstone of the Old Testament: the land called Nod.

From Cain's rebellion to Paul's confrontation with Peter (Galatians 2:11–14), Scripture indicates men are to be held accountable to other men. Surely every person is accountable to God for his actions, but men need relationships with other men in which they are held accountable for what they do.

We need one another. God created us to live in community. One critical dynamic of community is accountability. It is a vital component of what it means to be brothers in Christ. I learned this truth at the beginning of my Christian life, thanks to loving, responsible Christian men. As a junior in college, I listened as a friend told me that authentic, biblical Christianity was not a religious system but a vital relationship with Jesus Christ. Thanks to him and a group of other young men who loved Christ and cared about me, after several months I realized I needed to dethrone ego and relinquish control of my life to Jesus Christ. Almost immediately I was surrounded by brothers who not only helped nurture my growth in Christ, but held me accountable for that growth.

I thought this pattern was the norm. After all, that was the way Jesus operated in the gospels. I was soon to discover that not only was this not the norm, but this kind of group accountability tragically is almost nonexistent in the body of Christ.

In the foreword of *Daily Disciplines for the Christian Man,* Vernon Grounds refers to a character he calls "Mr. Typical Evangelical." Such a man, Grounds argues, lacks a meaningful daily strategy to live a vital spiritual life. Let me suggest that developing effective sources of accountability is one critical dynamic of the vital spiritual life.

According to *Websters New World Dictionary,* the primary definition of the adjective *accountable* is "responsible; liable." The linguistic root of the word *accountable* is "account" in the sense of analyzing, explaining, and being held open to the critique of one's behavior.

Accountability comes in various shapes and sizes. Let's look at three relationships that God has designed to be sources of biblical accountability.

Accountability to God

Authentic Christian faith is intended to be a vital relationship with the living God. At the heart of this relationship you must always remember two foundational truths: (1) There is a God. (2) I am not Him!

Men always laugh when I declare those truths, but in many ways they are much more profound than humorous. There is a God, and I am not Him. He is holy, and I am—well, let's say, not! He is perfect and I am flawed. He makes the rules; I play by them (and often break them). When the day is done, ultimately I must give account to Him.

David, a shepherd who later became king of Israel, was a man much like you and me. After years of living as "a man after God's own heart," he really blew it. He committed adultery with Bathsheba and arranged to have her husband, Uriah, murdered to cover up his sin. David finally got honest with God after the prophet Nathan (relentless accountability was his strong suit) pointed the finger at him and declared, "You are the man" (see 2 Samuel 12:7–10). David repented and eventually wrote a song that appears in our Bible as Psalm 51. In this psalm David affirms to God, "Against You, You only have I sinned" (Psalm 51:4).

That might surprise you. You might be thinking, *What about Uriah the Hittite?* What David discovered in this incident was that his ultimate accountability was to God, not to Urriah. In every model of accountability we must begin with this principle: As men we always stand accountable before God.

This vertical accountability is enhanced by a number of horizontal relationships God has designed to help keep us on track.

Accountability to Christian Men

Home from college during spring break, I drove by my girlfriend's house and saw the old, yellow Porsche parked in the driveway. I still liked her a lot, and the Porsche confirmed the rumors. My old flame had become a "Jesus freak."

Some of my old school friends had too, but I really was uncomfortable because Sally (not her real name) had also become a Christian. (I had no idea what "Christian" even meant.) Even worse, she was actually dating the youth minister who was leading this new religious movement that several of my old schoolmates were caught up in. His name was Richard Beach. The Porsche was his, and so was my old girlfriend.

I met Rich on the 4th of July, 1970. I was with a group of friends who had gone to a party at an abandoned rock quarry outside Kansas City. It was a notorious hangout for the "turn on, tune in, and drop out" crowd. Upon arriving at the quarry I was delighted to see a rock band, complete with generators, ready to crank up the tunes. Everyone gathered around to hear the band play. When the band finished, Rich stood and addressed the crowd. Though this was a secular band and the crowd could have been rowdy, he stood up and talked about Jesus Christ. After giving a brief evangelistic message, he invited anyone who wanted to talk further to stick around for a while. For the next forty-five minutes Rich and I talked about what it meant to be a Christian.

This incident set the stage for my conversion to Christ. I had no idea that by the next time the 4th of July rolled around, Rich Beach would have become the best friend I had ever had. He would teach me what it meant to have a Christian brother who loved you and earned the right to hold you accountable. Neither one of us ended up with my old girlfriend, but God gave me a friendship that has lasted more than twenty years.

Over the next few months I seriously wrestled with spiritual issues. What would it mean to commit my life to Christ? I began to count the cost. I thought I could probably handle most of the required changes, but without a doubt, the biggest crisis I faced was the fear that I would lose all my friends.

One Saturday morning a few months later I showed up to play football with Rich and some of the young men from Colonial Presbyterian Church against another church team. During the game a "fight"—really a wrestling match—broke out between the two church teams about a play. I found myself looking at all these guys rolling around on the ground, wrestling with each other. I remember thinking to myself, "I think I could be a Christian!" During the following week I invited Jesus Christ into my life to be my personal Lord and Savior.

I don't believe it always happens this way, but for me, receiving Christ did mean the loss of many old friends. But with the loss of my old friends God brought into my life a small group of Christian guys who began to teach me what it's like to have Christian friendships. Part of what I learned was the role accountability plays among the brothers. I began to understand what the Scripture meant when it said, "As iron sharpens iron, so one man sharpens another" (Proverbs 27:17).

When I think about the role accountability has played in my life, I am reminded of the TV show "Cheers." During the first season of the show, I was walking through the family room when I heard the words to the theme song for the first time. Those words really hit home. They described a place to go when life is getting you down, a place "where everybody knows your name," a place where people express their common struggles and are genuinely glad you are there. *How tragic to waste such a great song on a TV show about a bar,* I thought as I listened. *This song should be the anthem of the church.*

Unfortunately, in the imperfect world in which we live, some bars actually might provide better fellowship than some of our churches. That is not the way it was intended to be. Fortunately, that was not my experience.

GRACE'S PLACE

Over the last twenty-plus years I have had the great blessing of having relationships with Christian brothers that have radically improved the quality of my life. These relationships have helped me realize how critical the brother-to-brother relationship is in becoming the kind of men that God intended for us to be. These men have taken me to what I call *Grace's Place.* Grace's Place is a spiritual reality where the theme song from "Cheers" finds fulfillment. It is a network of relationships that are always there when times are tough, a place where a small group of men know your name and are "always glad you came," as the TV lyrics say. Grace's Place is a metaphor for the dynamics of accountability relationships within the fellowship of the brothers.

The type of relationship it takes to have a Grace's Place experience in your life is called *fellowship* in the New Testament. *Fellowship* is our English translation of the Greek word *koinonia. Koinonia* means "a sharing in common." Authentic fellowship is a sharing of our life with another person who among other things has earned the right to hold us accountable. For men, this fellowship, on its deepest spiritual level, includes disclosure of our fears, failures, and hopes, as well as our successes.

Add to that, being accountable for spiritual, social, and emotional change, and you have an accountability relationship.

This kind of relationship requires the cultivation of several critical qualities. Without these qualities it is almost impossible for authentic, spiritual accountability to develop.

QUALITY ONE: UNCONDITIONAL LOVE

Accountability that impacts our lives with the life-changing power of the Spirit of God occurs within the context of relationships built on the foundation of God's unconditional love. Before becoming a Christian I had never experienced an unconditional friendship. What often pass for friendships in our culture are actually relationships of convenience and mutual usefulness. We develop these "friendships" based on what someone can do for us or how the relationship will help us get ahead in the rat race. Most of these relationships are highly conditional.

People must earn the right to hold you accountable; that right comes when you sense their unconditional acceptance of you. Then trust is possible. A relationship based on unconditional love is a firm foundation for an accountability relationship.

Be wary of friendships that are based on performance or appearances. In high school and college I wanted to be friends with people who would help me look good (a very difficult task at the time). I wanted to run around with the "in group" and the "sharp" kids so that I would be identified with them. If someone didn't measure up to my criteria in these areas I didn't have time or energy for him. I see the same dynamic at work every day in adult life. People measure and evaluate each other by skin color, financial statements, and club memberships. When someone doesn't meet our criteria for "friendship" we effectively eliminate him from our personal universe.

This approach to relationships is incredibly destructive! Not only is it destructive for the person who doesn't quite measure up to our standards, but this type of behavior is destructive to our own inner life. It is a vivid exercise in human self-centeredness.

In your relationships with Christian brothers, real friends will like you for who you are. In my own relationships with Christian men, I had little to offer them that would have improved their social standing. As a matter of fact, they couldn't have cared less about that kind of thing. Their whole approach to our relationship was one of unconditional love. They were committed to my highest welfare and spiritual growth. They became human vehicles through whom the unconditional love of Christ was expressed. They earned the right to hold me accountable.

QUALITY TWO: AVAILABILITY

I have had the good fortune of having many male relationships that rest on unconditional love, but my friendship with Bo Mitchell was one of a kind, for he changed the course of my life. Bo demonstrated the quality of availability; he was always there to offer help.

Bo was a successful young businessman when we met in the spring of 1980. We teamed up to develop a ministry to nonchurched businessmen and their families. For more than ten years Bo and I were able to address men's retreats around the nation on the subject of biblical priorities.

In the early days of our friendship Bo used to say, "Everything I have is yours, except my wife." He meant it. If my car broke down, Bo considered it to be his problem. When I couldn't find a publisher for my first book, Bo put up the money to self-publish the book. Together we became Full Court Press. When Allison and I were going through marital struggles, Bo called every day and encouraged me to hang in there.

Bo taught me and modeled for me the quality of availability. Over the years I've had the opportunity to reciprocate in small ways. When the economy of Denver went into a tailspin Bo lost virtually everything. On several occasions Allison and I have made our resources available to help Bo make it through his tough times. Friendship begins to get very gutsy at these levels.

When my son was in surgery, Bo was there. When his wife, Gari, was in surgery, I was there. That's what authentic friendship looks like. It requires a commitment of availability of our time, energy, and resources. Few friendships develop this level of commitment. When availability is present, accountability becomes empowered. You are willing to be accountable to someone who is willing to sacrifice and help you.

QUALITY THREE: HONESTY

Authentic accountability requires honesty. In each of the relationships I've mentioned there has been one common link: a commitment to honesty. When I'm having a tough time and need someone to talk to I know that I can be honest with these friends. I tell them what is really going on in my gut and they tell me the same. In John Wesley's class meetings every member was required to tell the other members of the group the "true state of his soul" at least once a week. In obedience to James 5:16, they confessed their sins to one another and prayed for one another. That takes honesty.

Honesty requires hard work, but it's a vital element in being accountable to another man. Sometimes honesty requires confronting our friend when we sense something is not quite right. This kind of honesty can produce conflict. Superficial relationships don't handle conflict well. But authentic friendships will grow through conflict. Remember: "As iron sharpens iron . . ." the book of Proverbs says. The image is of two swords crashing against each other and creating a friction that literally rubs off each's rough edges. It is often the fear of the difficulty of this friction that keeps many men from entering accountable relationships.

None of us likes to be told that he is wrong. The natural response to criticism is defensiveness and rationalization. Recently I was reminded of these realities the hard way.

I have a passion for reaching nonbelievers; I remember what it was like to be one. As a result I work hard to identify and communicate in a way that I believe will crack their defense systems and enable them to honestly consider Christ. Both of these characteristics tend to get me in hot water on occasion with more traditional members of the church family.

On a Friday evening in December I spoke to a group of 6,000 men and women. I gave a message so unconventional and nontraditional that it "pushed the envelope" to the limits. This particular Friday evening happened to fall on the night before Christmas.

As I prepared and then delivered this message I was totally focused on the hard-core non-Christian (like I used to be) who tends to show up only on Christmas Eve (like I did). In my zeal to communicate with this group, I was oblivious to how my message would be received by the more traditional people sitting in the pew who have certain expectations of what Christmas Eve ought to be like.

For the next few weeks I received a flood of letters suggesting everything from my immediate release so I could "pursue my giftedness elsewhere" to my burning at the stake. Some of the criticism was constructive. Some was malicious and abusive. I was wounded and angered at first by the latter. But in my heart I wanted God to use this situation to teach me and mold me.

I am an ordained Presbyterian minister (a fact that makes me believe God must surely have a tremendous sense of humor). As such, I am organizationally accountable to a board of elders. Because I trust these men and women, I am relationally accountable to them also. "The Nightmare After Christmas" (the prophetic title of my Christmas Eve message) became a time when my entire life and ministry were scrutinized by this group. Some of their conclusions were painful.

Proverbs reminds us, "Faithful are the wounds of a friend" (27:6). None of us likes pain. We spend most of our lives avoiding it at all cost. Accountability can be painful. But when the pain is caused by the critique of someone who authentically cares for us, it can have a powerful effect in our lives. We need not fear this kind of pain. Such honesty, given in love, will always be beneficial.

Conversely, there is a pain that is not so positive. It is caused by betrayal. I felt some of this pain in my situation. Some whom I would have hoped would have been supportive used the opportunity to strike a blow. Jesus knew this pain as He dipped the bread and handed it to Judas. But I am convinced that God can use even the pain of betrayal to mold us into His men and accomplish His redemptive purposes. Sometimes we avoid accountability because we fear betrayal. Ironically, when we have developed accountability relationships with a few trusted friends we actually free ourselves from the tyranny of the fickle opinions of the masses.

Proverbs also teaches, "A friend loves at all times, and a brother is born for adversity" (17:17). In the midst of this personal crisis it was the love and honesty of a few friends that enabled me to sort the wheat from the chaff and hear what God was saying to me. These brothers encouraged and enabled me to take steps to seek to correct the issues raised by this incident.

If you aren't accountable to somebody, you will end up feeling accountable to everybody. If you are willing to take the risk and develop relationships that lead to accountability, you will discover that the risk is well worth the benefit.

It seems all too often these days that I hear of Christian leaders who have fallen into sin and lost their ministry, or at least the sense of integrity that accompanied their ministry. I have the suspicion that these are men whose success has led to a degree of isolation. In isolation no one knew what was really going on in their lives. They didn't have friends with whom they could be truly honest. That is tragic. We all need the honesty that characterizes authentic Christian brotherhood. Without honesty, accountability is a sham.

QUALITY FOUR: CONFIDENTIALITY

An open and honest friendship requires a high level of trust. If I am going to share my struggles with a buddy to whom I have given the right to hold me accountable, I need to have the confidence that what I share is not going to appear as a headline in tomorrow's *National Enquirer.*

By nature most people are not very good in this area of confidentiality. Nothing kills the honesty in a relationship like a breach of confidence. Loose lips not only sink ships, they also sink fellowships. True friends know how to keep their mouths shut and hold confidences in confidence. If I am going to be accountable to you, I need to know I can trust you.

QUALITY FIVE: CONSISTENT TIME TOGETHER

Developing accountability relationships requires the investment of time and energy. The friends I have grown close to are the ones I spend time with. I believe the reason many people fail to develop accountability is that they fail to plan regular times of fellowship into their schedules.

I live in a busy metropolitan area. My life is filled with activity. I have more opportunities than time. Therefore, I have to make choices about how I am going to spend my time. Everyone I know is busy. Indeed, life in America is busy. Unfortunately, much of the time we are busy attending to the urgent while the truly important gets neglected.

I know that I need regular time alone with Allison, so I schedule it. I also need regular time with my children, Stephanie and Baker, so I plan it. But I have also learned that I need regular time with a small group of men who provide for me a Grace's Place experience. I have learned to prioritize this time into my schedule. It takes quality time of consistent regularity to build authentic accountability.

QUALITY SIX: PRAYER

I want the friends who hold me accountable to be men of prayer. Authentic brothers pray for one another. I have no greater gift to give a buddy than my intercession on his behalf in the presence of the living God.

In the last several years I have experienced a renaissance in this area of my spiritual life. I try to spend a significant amount of time daily in prayer. A notebook helps guide my time and remind me of the issues I need to talk to God about. One section of the notebook contains a list of the friends I am praying for, and when we meet, everyone tells the others the needs and issues of his life. As we share our needs, we pray for one another, and, of course, I will recall those needs later when I open the notebook for prayer.

Over the years I have seen God do exciting things in response to the prayers of my friends. As I pray for them, and as they pray for me, our friendships deepen and accountability becomes an inherent dimension of the relationship. If I am going to take a role in holding a brother accountable, I also must be committed to praying for and with that brother about the very issues we share together.

PROACTIVE ACCOUNTABILITY

Perhaps you have never had the kind of relationship that leads to accountability. Maybe you are thinking that you could never have a friendship like this. Let me assure you, you can. These kinds of relationships can take place when we are active in developing accountability relationships. In fact we must be proactive, anticipating and initiating on our own.

I have learned a very important lesson in this regard. My friendships with Rich and Bo developed very naturally. I didn't have to invest much energy to make them happen. Then a strange thing occurred. I began to lose touch with these friends. Rich was living in another city, which made consistent time together impossible. Bo had teamed up with a few other men to develop several new ministries. We were connecting sporadically. I began feeling lonely and isolated, like many men feel.

I wish I could tell you that I was wise enough and exhibited the initiative to work on this area of need, but that is not quite how it happened. God, in His grace, was getting ready to teach me a lesson. I did take one highly proactive step. I began to pray that God would help me develop some new friendships. I believe that what happened was a direct answer to those prayers.

Without giving much thought to the friendship implications of my actions, I started to think about forming a discipleship group with several men. These were guys who I wanted to get to know better but rarely scheduled the time to do so. Several of these men were new Christians who I thought I might be able to help in the process of spiritual growth. I prayed about each person I wanted to get to know better and then began to call to see if they would be interested in being part of a group. Every man that God had placed on my heart responded enthusiastically.

We began meeting together in September 1990. Our commitment was to meet regularly, every other week during the lunch hour. Our objective was to tackle a discipleship program developed by The Navigators. The 2:7 Series requires a commitment to memorize Scripture, cultivate a daily discipline of Bible study and prayer, and work to develop basic skills in ministry. The men were open to such a commitment.

As our group spent time together, an exciting chemistry evolved. Along with accomplishing the tasks we had committed ourselves to, a spirit of camaraderie rapidly began to develop among the members of the group. Although I had the job of providing leadership for the group, I didn't look at our times together as work. I began to look forward to our meetings as a time to be with good friends.

One of the "grace" dimensions of the group was the choice of Thursday as our meeting day. My teaching load is heavily weighted on the front end of the week. I teach a Bible study for about 250 businessmen very early on Tuesday mornings. On Wednesday nights I teach another Bible study where often more than 1,000 men and women attend. These events are emotionally, physically, and spiritually draining. By Thursday, I usually feel worn out. Shortly after our group started to meet I began to experience serious emotional letdowns on Thursdays. I also was going through a period of discouragement rooted in some failed expectations about our Wednesday night group. Thursdays were becoming very difficult.

I revealed the struggle I was going through to the group. The men rallied to my side. They became a tremendous source of support as I worked through this time of difficulty. The group was rapidly developing all the qualities of authentic biblical fellowship.

We met together regularly in a spirit of unconditional love to help each other grow spiritually. We made ourselves available to each other and sought to be there for members of the group who were having a tough time. We were learning to be open and honest with each other. We held each other accountable for spiritual growth and lovingly yet firmly encouraged each other. We prayed for and with each other. We goofed off and had fun together too!

Significantly, this was an *intentional group.* It didn't happen naturally. It was planned and pursued on the basis of choice and action. The result was the creation of relationships where accountability could take place. If you are ready to become accountable, you also have the ability to initiate action to develop these kinds of relationships with a small group of brothers.

You might already have existing friendships that simply require a little work to develop into accountability relationships. You might need to be the "point man" who gets the ball rolling. Let me suggest a few steps you could take.

Begin by asking God to give you relationships where accountability can take place. Ask Him to show you a few men you might begin to meet together with on a regular basis. Maybe there is a group of men you have been wanting to get to know better who could become such a group.

Once you have a sense of who you might want to meet with, initiate contact. You might be surprised that the very men God has placed on your heart have also been looking for accountability relationships. Spend some time together talking about what you need and expect out of this kind of friendship.

Some readers may have tried being in a group before and didn't have such a great experience. Let me assure you that you are not alone. There are good groups and bad groups. I have been in both! There also is a kind of mysterious chemistry that works in some relationships and doesn't in others. My advice is don't give up. It might take a few attempts before you find a group that works for you.

You also may have had an experience that wasn't quite right for your personality and temperament. The good news is that there isn't only one way to accomplish this objective. Some men love being in a group of six or seven brothers. Others are wired in such a way that they are only comfortable with one or two other men. Some men love praying aloud in groups and hardly ever get alone with God in the "prayer closet." Others are much more comfortable getting alone and seeking God in solitude. The key is to find what works for you and then pursue it. If you are willing to work at this kind of relationship, the rewards can be great. For specific steps and guidelines for starting a group see Pete Richardson's practical booklet, *Why*

Christian Men Need Each Other, part of this Men of Integrity series.

Accountability to Your Mate

If you are married, accountability begins on the home front. In fact, built-in accountability is one of the added bonuses of a solid marriage. Some men reading may think that if they have accountability to men, that's sufficient. But accountability needs to begin at home. Don't get involved in a men's movement toward accountability in order to escape your marriage. Instead, use the presence of your wife to both develop your friendship and deepen your marriage tie.

Of course, if your marriage isn't on solid ground, being accountable to your wife won't work, for accountability requires honesty and unconditional love, as we noted earlier. If your marriage seems shaky or is even dysfunctional, you are missing a God-given opportunity to confide to a quality friend. Work on strengthening the relationship first; then a solid accountability relationship will be yours.

LOGIC VERSUS INTUITION

There are two dimensions of accountability in marriage that you will find in no other relationship. The first has to do with the way God has designed men and women. Researchers have found that a person's ability to reason resides primarily in the left hemisphere of the brain, and they theorize that most men are "left-brain" dominant. Certainly I am "left-brain" dominant. I am so logical in my approach to life that I have even rationally analyzed my approach and found it to be the superior way. Most men are quite a bit like me in this emphasis on reasoning to tackle issues.

There is only one small problem with the logical approach: Life isn't always logical.

Ali (my favorite name for Allison) is extremely intuitive. Most women are. I lead with my head; she leads with her heart. Many, *many* times I have "figured something out," only to have Ali tell me she doesn't think it "feels right." That phrase used to drive me crazy. After learning the hard way that she is usually sensing something I am oblivious to, I have come to trust her heart as much as my head.

I remember one of those times when my wife was right—again. We had an argument after Ali "critiqued" one of my brilliant ideas. She was holding me accountable and I didn't like it. But after listening, I had to admit to her that she was right. After twenty years of wedded bliss I think Ali and I are finally getting to the point where we are able to hold each other accountable without making frequent visits to our favorite marriage counselor.

KEEPING US HONEST

The second benefit of accountability in marriage is the absolute reality of the relationship. At twenty-one I thought I was a spiritual giant. Then I got married. Marriage has a way of bringing out the best and worst in a man. You see, I am quite skilled at what I call "blowing smoke." I can fool my buddies and brothers, but I can't fool my wife. She really knows me. She knows when I am living in the flesh and when I'm walking in the Spirit.

Honesty is not an option in our marriage; it is built-in. For most couples, after a period of time the wife begins to understand well the husband's tone of voice, his good days and bad days, and his strengths and weaknesses. When we as husbands can tap into their perceptions to learn about ourselves, we find our wives to be valuable resources indeed.

AN ATTITUDE OF SUBMISSION

Along with these two benefits, there are also two problems with true accountability, husband to wife.

The first is that it requires submission on the man's part to the input of his wife. For some men, this is a real problem. It was for me. God has had to work in my heart to enable me to submit to my wife.

I know what you are thinking: *The Bible says she is supposed to be in submission to me!* True, but it also says we are to submit to our wives!

The classic text on submission is found in Ephesians 5. Most men like to begin in verse 22 where wives are told to "submit to [their] husbands as to the Lord." I have seen some amazing distortions of God's plan for marriage based upon this text. In the original language the verb "submit" does not even appear in verse 22. The verse is grammatically dependent upon the participle in verse 21. This verse says "submitting to one another in reverence for Christ." Who is the "one another"? Verses 22–33 tell us: husbands and wives. The manner in which submission is worked out differs for men and women, but there can be no doubt that it is commanded for both.

Developing this kind of relationship with your wife will not only enhance your spiritual life, but it will transform your marriage. You will begin to understand why you can never seem to change her. You aren't supposed to! You are supposed to listen carefully to her and allow her to be the "suitable companion" God created her to be. That is the meaning of the Hebrew in Genesis 2 usually translated "helpmate" (but sometimes interpreted by the male of the species as "household slave").

I am a big believer in divine sovereignty and providence. I believe that before the foundation of the world God knew me (see Ephesians 1:4). I also believe that before the foundation of the world He knew what kind of wife I needed to become the man He intended me to be. I believe He created Ali to be my companion and partner in this world. I believe He engineered the circumstances of our lives to make sure we ended up together. He didn't make any mistakes. She is the right woman and all her characteristics are divinely designed to complement mine.

I believe that what is true of Ali and me is also true of every married Christian couple. You are married to God's most precious gift to you, next to His Son. Are you allowing her to play the role in your life God intended? Are you letting yourself be accountable to your wife?

LIMITATIONS

There is a second problem with the accountability possible in the marriage relationship: It has its limitations. As wonderful as the feminine intuitive perspective is, it often is inadequate by itself. That should not be surprising; just as there are limits to what men can do for us in an accountability relationship, so there are limits to what our wives can do. Only God can be counted on to know, understand, and accept all we are.

Certain issues cannot be addressed with our wives, either because of the nature of the topic or the need for another, masculine perspective. That is why men need other men.

Closer than a Brother

Certainly the relationships we can have with men are special. You may even hook up with another man in a distinct friendship that, like that of David and Jonathan, lets the two of you become "one in spirit" (1 Samuel 18:1). Perhaps it was the stories David told to his son Solomon about his friendship with Jonathan that led Solomon to write, "There is a friend who sticks closer than a brother" (Proverbs 18:24). We have no record in Scripture that Solomon himself had such a friendship. Few men do. But it is possible for all men to have such a friendship, if they are willing to develop the qualities listed earlier and to devote time to the friendship.

For more than twenty years now I have had one unique relationship that has been like that of David and his friend Jonathan. Rich Beach has been that kind of friend to me. When I hurt he hurts; when he hurts I hurt. When I need counsel I go to him; when he needs counsel he comes to me. When he sat in the doctor's office awaiting the results of a prostate biopsy I was with him. When I struggled with the pain of intense criticism concerning my ministry, he was there. I never had a brother, but Rich has been one—and more.

I believe that the secret to our friendship is that we have worked at the relationship for more than twenty years. Every principle mentioned in this booklet has been put into practice and allowed to mature. By the grace of God we have planted good seed for many years, and we now share the joy of reaping the harvest.

I don't mention this to evoke your envy. Well, maybe I do. I wish you envied our relationship enough to desire one like it for yourself. I write this to tell you that God has a "Rich" for your life. You probably won't find him without a little proactive energy on your part. But if you're willing to work at developing accountability at this level, you can experience what it means to have a friend who is closer than a brother.

If you have such a man in your life, thank him for his loyalty and tell him what he means to you. If you don't, work developing such a friendship—a friendship in which another man holds you accountable and supports you with unconditional love. Then one day you will look back and see the blessings and growth God has brought to your spiritual life because you were a man who became accountable.

Moody Press, a ministry of the Moody Bible Institute, is designed for education, evangelization, and edification. If we may assist you in knowing more about Christ and the Christian life, please write us without obligation: Moody Press, c/o MLM, Chicago, Illinois 60610.